The Fantastic
Rainy Day Book

ANGELA WILKES

For Sam, Rose, Charlotte, Billy, Laurence, Sam, and Barney.

Designer Jane Bull
Photographer Dave King
Home Economist Janie Suthering

Project Editor Helen Drew
Text Designers Adrienne Hutchinson,
Katie Poyner, and Cheryl Telfer
Managing Editor Jane Yorke
Managing Art Editor Gillian Allan
US Editor Camela Decaire

First American Edition, 1995
8 10 9 7
First published in the United States by
DK Publishing Inc., 95 Madison Avenue
New York, New York 10016
Copyright © 1995 Dorling Kindersley Limited, London
Text copyright © 1995 Angela Wilkes

Visit us on the World Wide Web at
http://www.dk.com

Library of Congress Cataloging-in-Publication Data

Wilkes, Angela.
The fantastic rainy day book / by Angela Wilkes. -- 1st American ed.
p. cm.
ISBN 1-56458-878-5
1. Handicraft--Juvenile literature. [1. Handicraft.]
I. Title
TT160. W5722 1995
745 . 5--dc20   94-36380
34261   AC
Color reproduction by Colourscan, Singapore
Printed and bound in Spain by Artes Gráficas Toledo, S.A.
D.L. TO: 1131-1999

Dorling Kindersley would like to thank Chris Branfield for jacket design, Andy Crawford for additional
photography, and Jonathan Buckley, Jane Horne, Jeannette Morton, Emma Patmore, and Chris Scollen
for their help in producing this book. Dorling Kindersley would also like to thank the following models
for appearing in this book: Holly Cowgill, Kelly Gomez, Emma Judson, Laurence King, Sam Priddy,
Taberge Ricketts, Darren Singh, Selena Singh, and Phoebe Thoms.

CONTENTS

COLLECTIONS

DRESSING UP

TREATS AND PRESENTS

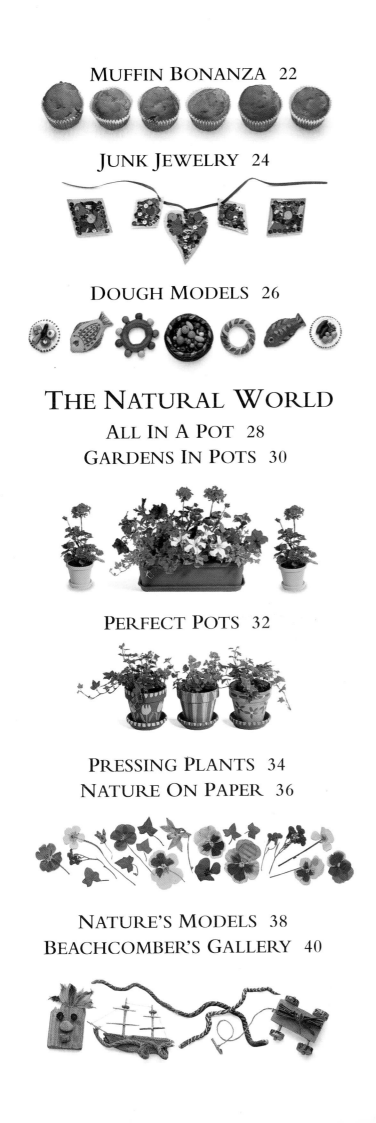

INTRODUCTION

This book will give you lots of inspiring ideas for things to make and do on a rainy day. But before you start, you must have the right materials. Here you can see lots of things used in this book. Save as many of them as you can and sort them into boxes, and they will be ready to transform into whatever you want! Remember – when you finish a project, put all your materials, equipment, and tools away in their boxes, and clean up any mess you have made.

Things to collect

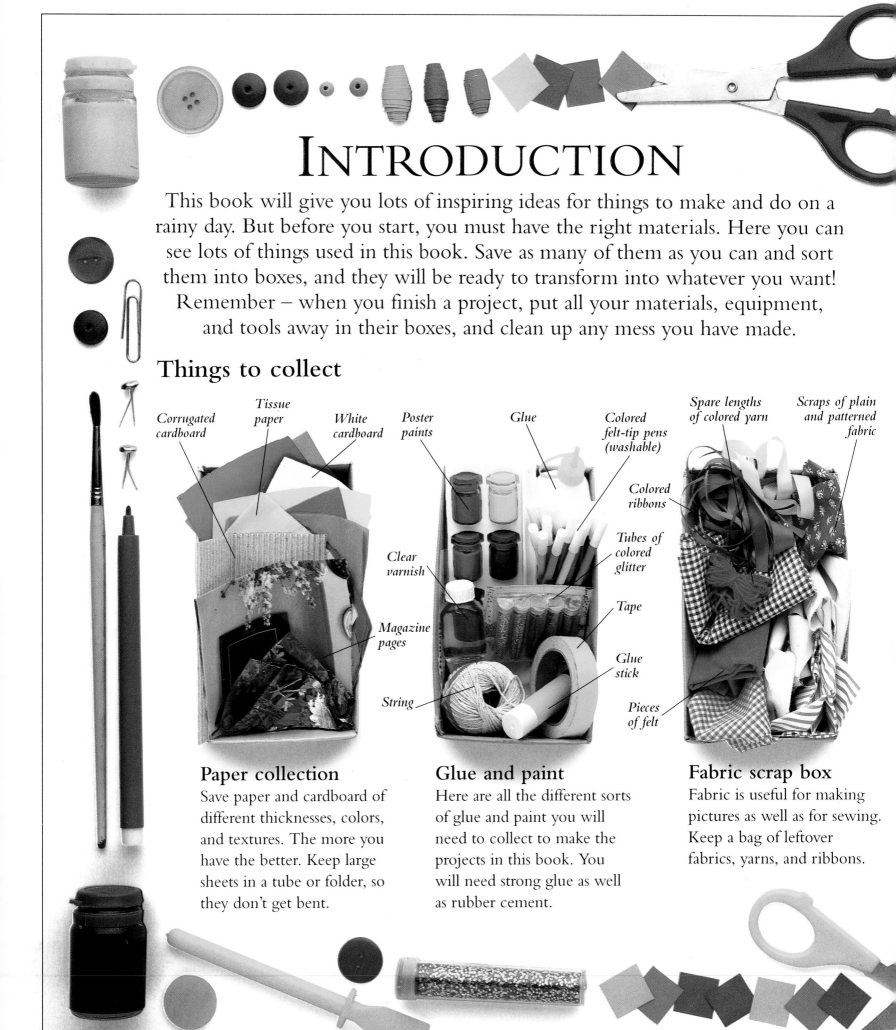

Corrugated cardboard

Tissue paper

White cardboard

Poster paints

Glue

Colored felt-tip pens (washable)

Spare lengths of colored yarn

Scraps of plain and patterned fabric

Colored ribbons

Clear varnish

Tubes of colored glitter

Magazine pages

Tape

String

Glue stick

Pieces of felt

Paper collection
Save paper and cardboard of different thicknesses, colors, and textures. The more you have the better. Keep large sheets in a tube or folder, so they don't get bent.

Glue and paint
Here are all the different sorts of glue and paint you will need to collect to make the projects in this book. You will need strong glue as well as rubber cement.

Fabric scrap box
Fabric is useful for making pictures as well as for sewing. Keep a bag of leftover fabrics, yarns, and ribbons.

Seeing stars

At the top of each page you will find a star symbol that tells you how long the most difficult project on each page takes.

One star
☆
Project takes an hour or less to complete.

Two stars
☆
☆
Project takes an afternoon to complete.

Three stars
☆
☆
☆
Project takes a day or more to complete.

Warning symbols

Look out for the red warning signs in the step-by-step instructions of some projects. Whenever you see one, you will need to ask an adult to help you.

The oven mitt symbol
When you see this symbol in a cooking project, put on oven mitts and ask an adult to help you.

The warning symbol
You will see this sign when sharp tools are used. Always ask an adult to help you.

Lots of colored sequins

Pins

Beads in lots of different shapes and colors

Plastic bottle tops

Small boxes

Twigs and pieces of wood

Feathers

Pinecones

Paper plates

Small cardboard tubes

Shells

Star stickers

Lentils and seeds

Egg carton

Interesting leaves

Paper clips

Small, brightly colored buttons

Straw and raffia

Treasure trove

These little things are perfect for adding details to the projects you make. Keep them safe in containers with lids.

Junk box

Save clean pieces of garbage for recycling into models and pictures. Cardboard boxes, packaging, cartons, and tubes of all shapes and sizes are very useful as well as plastic lids and tops.

Nature box

The nicest things to collect are the things you find out on walks in a park, in a forest, or along a beach. As you walk, always keep an eye out for unusual and interesting objects.

MAKING PICTURES

One of the best ways to spend a rainy day is making pictures. You don't even have to be good at drawing because you can produce brilliant mosaics and collages from paper, seeds, pasta, magazine photographs, scraps of fabric, and glue. Below you can see how to make some different sorts of pictures. Turn the page to see the finished works of art and to find out how to frame them.

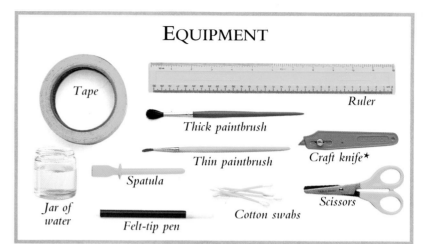

EQUIPMENT

Tape

Ruler

Thick paintbrush

Thin paintbrush

Craft knife★

Spatula

Jar of water

Felt-tip pen

Cotton swabs

Scissors

You will need

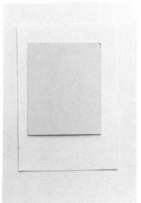

Different types of thick white paper

Scraps of fabric

Pages torn out of old magazines

Colored paper

Glue with a nozzle

Dried beans, seeds, and pasta

Smooth stones and pebbles

Clear varnish

Poster paints

Glue stick

Corrugated cardboard

Mosaic picture

1 Mosaics look best with simple shapes and patterns. Start by drawing an outline of your picture on a piece of thick white paper.

2 Choose the colors you want to use in your picture. Then cut pages in these colors out of magazines and tear them into small squares.

3 Spread glue on part of the picture and stick down the squares. Start with the background and work in rows from the top downward.

★ *Always ask an adult to help you use a craft knife.*

Paper or fabric pictures

1 Choose a piece of paper or fabric for the background and glue it onto thick paper. Then glue strips of paper or fabric around the border.

2 Tear out paper shapes for the main image. Arrange them on the background until you are happy with the design. Then glue them in place.

3 Add details to your pictures with smaller pieces of paper. Arrange the pieces on the picture before you glue them in position.

Painted pebbles

1 Choose smooth pebbles or stones. Wash them and let them dry. Paint the pebbles all over with a thick coat of white paint and let them dry.

2 Now paint a picture on each stone. Paint the larger areas of color first and let them dry before painting the smaller details, with a fine brush, on top.

3 When the paint has dried, brush each pebble with clear varnish and let it dry. This helps prevent paint chipping.

Seed collage

1 Sort lots of different-colored seeds, dried beans, and pasta. Draw an outline of your picture on a piece of thick white paper.

2 Spread glue on part of the picture and carefully sprinkle some beans or seeds on top. Push them into place with the hard end of a paintbrush.

3 Continue sticking on seeds until the picture is finished. Add small details with lines of beans or seeds, or by breaking off small pieces of pasta.

PICTURE GALLERY

Making a frame

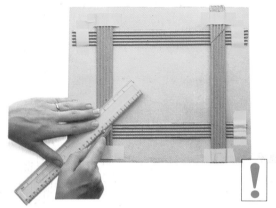

1 Cut four long strips of corrugated cardboard each about 1½ in. (3 cm) wide. Tape them together, as shown, to fit the picture you are framing.

2 Ask an adult to score the edges of the cardboard strips diagonally, as shown. Cut the strips along the score lines. Then peel off the tape.

3 Turn the frame over and tape the edges together. Paint and varnish the front of the frame, then tape your picture to the back of the frame.

Coral fish mosaic

Painted corrugated cardboard frame

On display

Here is a gallery of all the different sorts of pictures you can make. The instructions on the left show you how to make frames for your pictures, or you could mount them on a sheet of colored paper or cardboard, instead.

Why not make frames for your paintings, too?

Seaside painting

Cloth cow

Fabric fun
Make a collection of different sorts of fabrics with interesting textures, colors, and patterns for your collages.

Marmalade cat

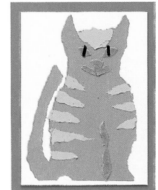

Tulip and bee

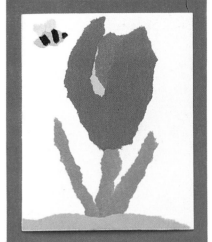

Torn paper pictures
These torn paper pictures are simple to make and they look stunning. Try making cards and gift tags in the same way.

You could even make fabric frames for your pictures.

Painted beach pebbles
These pebbles have a seaside theme. The shapes of your pebbles may suggest other ideas. The stones make fun paperweights.

Duck in the snow

Boat at sea

Beach crab

Shoal of fish

Sun and sea

Orange paper mount

Seed street collage

PAINTED FACES

You can have great fun with your friends painting each other's faces. You can become a tiger, a clown, or anything you want! Look at pictures in books and magazines for ideas, and then copy the details when you paint. The best face paints are water-based ones, which are easy to apply and quickly wash off afterward. You can blend face colors together to make new shades, just as you do with watercolor paints.

You will need

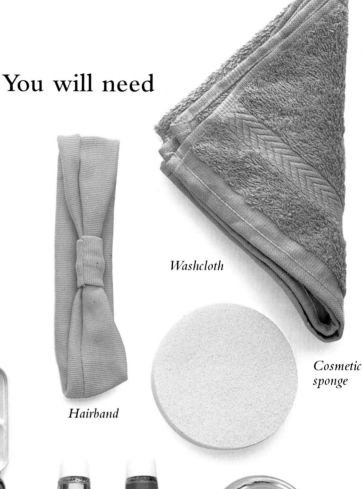

Washcloth

Cosmetic sponge

Hairband

Tubes of glitter paint for faces

Jar of water

Water-based face paints

Fine paintbrush

Broader, flat paintbrush

Applying a base

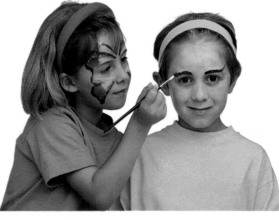

Put a hairband on your model. Wet the sponge and squeeze it out so it is just damp. Rub it gently in the base color and then sponge the paint evenly over the face.

Adding the detail

Allow the base color to dry. Then paint on details, using the face paints like normal paints. Use the flat brush for large areas of color and the fine brush for details.

Cleaning up

Wipe off the face paints with soap and water and a clean washcloth. Don't let soap get in the eyes.

Happy clown

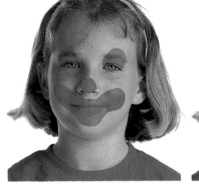

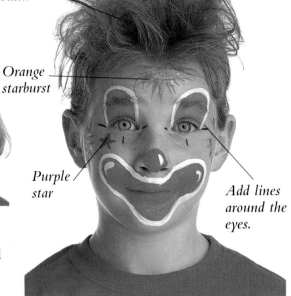

1 This face doesn't need a base. Paint two green ovals over the eyelids and eyebrows.

2 Then paint on a large red mouth and a red circle on the end of the nose.

3 Paint white outlines around the eyes and mouth and add white highlights where shown.

Butterfly face

Line of glitter

Antenna

Wing

1 With the fine brush, paint on the outline of a butterfly's wings and antennae.

2 Then paint in patches of color inside the wing outline with the flat brush.

3 Paint smaller areas of color with the fine brush. Add lines of glitter paint where shown.

Terrible tiger

Thick black and white tiger stripes

Thin black whiskers

White furry muzzle

1 Sponge yellow around the middle of the face and orange around the edges.

2 Then paint on feathery white eyes and a muzzle, and fan them out at the edges.

3 Paint a black mouth and nose. Add black lines around the eyes and spots on the muzzle.

11

QUICK DISGUISES

With a little imagination and some bits and pieces of scraps, you can put together a quick disguise and turn yourself into another person. You could be a detective, a famous movie star, or even Santa Claus. Change your clothes and put on a hat – no one will know who you really are.

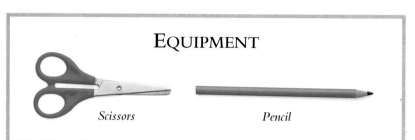

EQUIPMENT

Scissors   *Pencil*

You will need

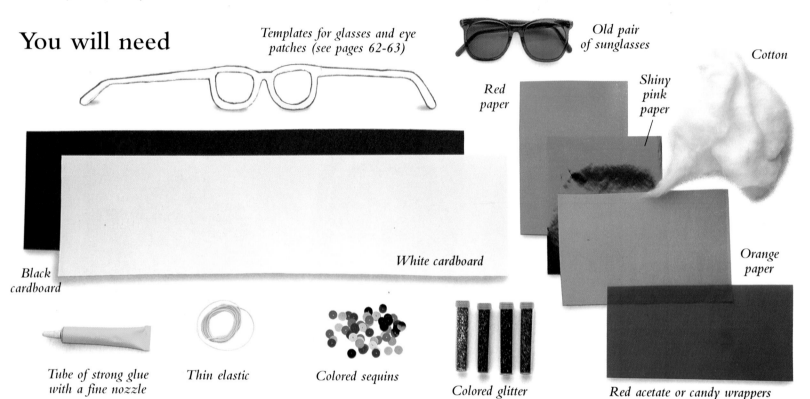

Templates for glasses and eye patches (see pages 62-63)

Old pair of sunglasses

Cotton

Red paper

Shiny pink paper

Black cardboard

White cardboard

Orange paper

Tube of strong glue with a fine nozzle

Thin elastic

Colored sequins

Colored glitter

Red acetate or candy wrappers

False noses

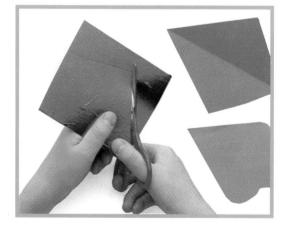

1 Make noses out of colored paper. Cut out a kite shape long enough to cover your nose and fold it in half. Or give the nose big, round nostrils.

2 Cut some elastic long enough to go around the back of your head. Thread it through two holes at the top of the nose and knot the ends.

Eye patches

Using the template on page 63, draw an eye patch on cardboard and cut it out. Glue on glitter. Attach a length of elastic as you did for the nose.

Detective disguise

Using the template on page 62, draw and cut out glasses from black cardboard. Glue on a false nose and add a cardboard mustache.

Movie star shades

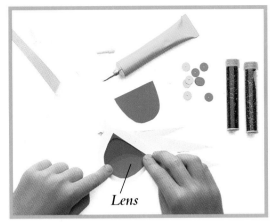

Lens

Use the glasses-with-wings template to make "shades." Glue lenses cut out of acetate to the back of the shades. Decorate the front with glitter.

Beard and mustache

Draw a beard and mustache on white cardboard and cut it out. Glue bits of cotton all over it. Tie elastic to the sides of the mustache, as for the nose.

Disguise kit

Here are the finished disguises. They are all really quick and easy to make. You can wear each one on its own, or combine two or three with a hat from page 15 for a total disguise.

False nose

Detective's disguise

Mustache

False nose

Old sunglasses

Instant disguise

Movie star shades

Sequin

Glitter frames

Acetate lens

Cotton

Pirate's eye patch

Glittery eye patch

Shiny false nose

Santa's beard

HATS GALORE

Hats come in all shapes and sizes and are great fun to dress up in. Put on a hat and you can pretend to be anyone you like. Here you can find out how to make three great hats from thick paper and a few extras. You will need to measure your head with a band of paper before you make the top hat and the boater.

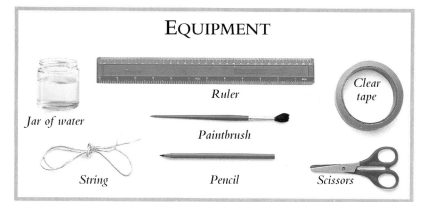

EQUIPMENT

Jar of water

Ruler

Clear tape

Paintbrush

String

Pencil

Scissors

You will need

Thick black, white, and yellow paper

Poster paints

Green, yellow, pink, and blue tissue paper

Green ribbon

Silky scarf

Measuring your head

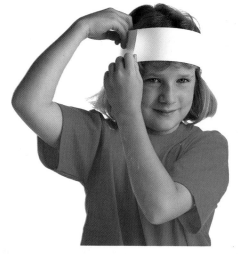

Cut a narrow strip of paper and wrap it around your head. Tape down the overlapping edge. This band shows the size of your head.

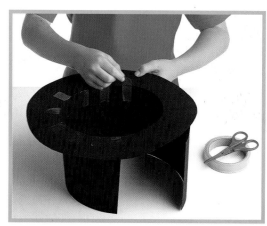

2 Cut a long length of paper about 6¼ in. (16 cm) tall. Roll it to fit inside the brim and tape it in place on the inside. Tape any overlapping edges.

Top hat

1 Tape the band onto black paper. Mark the inside edge of the band and draw a circle 2 in. (5 cm) out from it. Remove it and cut around both circles.

Boater

Make a boater 3 in. (7.5 cm) tall out of white paper, as for the top hat. Tape the circle cut from inside the brim to the top of the hat. Then paint the hat.

Sun hat

1 To make the brim, draw a circle 7 in. (17 cm) across, as shown on page 60, and a second one, 16½ in. (42 cm) across, around it. Cut out the circles.

2 Fold a sheet of tissue paper in half and gently push it into the hole, as shown. Trim off the rough edges and tape the tissue paper inside the brim.

3 Tape a scarf across the tissue paper, as shown. Scrunch squares of tissue paper into flowers and tape them around the brim of the hat.

Hat parade

And here are all the featured hats, ready to wear. Try making other styles, like a witch's hat, a crown, or even a huge sombrero to complete your dressing up wardrobe.

Jolly boater

Hat painted with broad yellow, red, and blue stripes

Top hat

Stick a band of shiny ribbon around the hat to hide the paper join.

Flowers made from scrunched up tissue paper

Sun hat

Tissue paper crown

Tuck a card under the ribbon to add a touch of color.

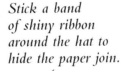

Tie the hat under your chin with the silky scarf.

Yellow paper brim

15

MAKING MASKS

Why not make a mask for a disguise party, for a special play, or just for dressing up? All the masks here cover your face to provide a complete disguise, and they are made from nothing more than paper plates and torn paper. Try copying the ideas shown here, or make up some masks of your own.

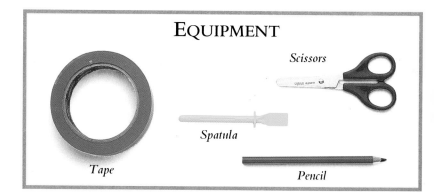

EQUIPMENT

Scissors

Spatula

Tape

Pencil

You will need

Colored paper

Large white paper plates

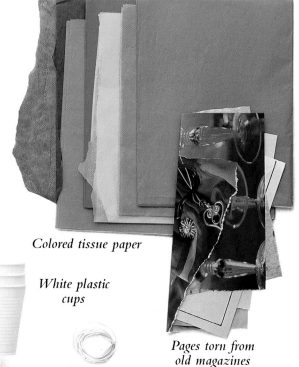

Colored tissue paper

Pages torn from old magazines

Rubber cement

Tubes of glitter

White crêpe paper

White plastic cups

Thin elastic

Red-eyed frog

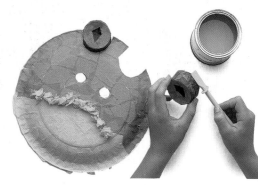

Cover a plate with green and yellow tissue paper. Cut two holes for nostrils. Make eyes from the bottom quarter of two cups covered with tissue paper.

Harlequin mask

Tear up diamonds of pink, yellow, and blue tissue paper and glue them onto a plate. Cut two diamonds for eyes and glue on a black paper mouth.

Leo lion

Cover a plate with torn orange magazine paper. Use strips of brown tissue paper for a mane and make the details of the face out of paper.

Polar bear

Draw around the bottom third of a cup in the middle of a plate. Cut out the circle and tape the cup into the hole. Cover both with balls of crêpe paper.

Bird of paradise

Make a beak from two folded triangles of yellow paper and glue them to a plate. Make a face with pink paper and glitter, and feathers from tissue paper.

Adding the elastic

Make a hole at each side of the mask. Cut some elastic long enough to go around your head and thread it through each hole. Tie a knot in each end.

Red-eyed frog

Stand-out cup eyes

Green tissue face

The nostrils are the eyeholes of the mask.

Scrunched paper mouth

Leo lion

Torn tissue paper mane

White paper whiskers

Black paper features

Polar bear

Black paper features

Muzzle made from a paper-covered cup

Ears made of pink paper and white crêpe paper balls

Mask collection

Here are all the finished masks. When you aren't wearing your masks, you can hang them up on your bedroom walls by the elastic.

Harlequin mask

Torn tissue diamonds

Black paper mouth

Bird of paradise

Glitter

Torn tissue crest

Blue tissue feathers

Yellow paper eyes

Folded yellow paper beak

MAKING CANDIES

What better way to spend a rainy afternoon than making some delicious candies to cheer everyone up? Here you can see everything you need to make peppermint creams, pink sugar mice, and marzipan bonbons. Then turn the page to see a mouthwatering array of the finished candies.

EQUIPMENT

For marzipan candies

Wooden spoon

Sharp knife

Sieve

Fork

Cookie cutters

Mixing bowl

Small bowl

Rolling pin

For peppermint creams

Fork

Whisk

Sieve

Sharp knife

Wooden spoon

Small saucepan

Baking sheet lined with waxed parchment

Mixing bowl

Small bowl

You will need

For marzipan candies

$^{1}/_{2}$ cup/ 4 oz/115 g confectioners' sugar

1 cup/ 8 oz/225 g ground almonds

Pink food coloring

$^{1}/_{2}$ cup/4 oz/115 g superfine sugar

Green food coloring

1 egg   An extra egg yolk

3 drops vanilla extract

1 teaspoon lemon juice

Licorice strings

Candied cherries

For peppermint creams and mice
(makes 16 creams and 4 mice)

2 oz/55 g dark chocolate

1 egg white

Pink food coloring

$1^{1}/_{2}$ cups/12 oz/340 g confectioners' sugar

Currants

A few drops peppermint extract

4 shelled peanuts

Licorice strings

Making the peppermint mixture

1 Put the egg white in the mixing bowl and beat it lightly with the whisk until it looks frothy, but stop before it becomes stiff.

2 Sift the confectioners' sugar into the bowl. Then stir it into the beaten egg white with a wooden spoon until the mixture is stiff.

3 Add a few drops of peppermint extract and knead it into the mixture. The more extract you add, the stronger the mints will taste.

Chocolate peppermint creams

4 Split half the mixture into 16 balls and put them on the lined baking sheet. Press them flat with a fork and leave them to set for 24 hours.

5 When the creams have set, break the chocolate into the small bowl. Set the bowl over a pan of simmering water until the chocolate melts.

6 Dip each peppermint cream into the melted chocolate, placing them all back on the baking sheet until the chocolate has solidified.

Sugar mice

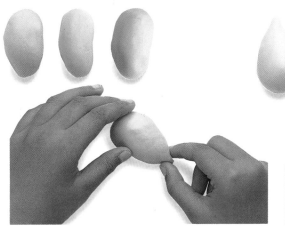

1 Knead a few drops of pink food coloring into the other half of the peppermint mixture, then break it into four equal-size pieces.

2 Shape each piece of the pink mixture into an oval shape with your hands, then pinch one end of each oval to make a pointed snout.

3 Add two currants to each oval to make eyes, and peanut halves to make ears. Cut small pieces of licorice string to make the tails.

Making the marzipan

1 Sift the confectioners' sugar into the mixing bowl to remove lumps. Add the superfine sugar and ground almonds, and stir them together.

2 Mix the egg, egg yolk, lemon juice, and vanilla extract together in the small bowl. Add them to the sugar mixture and mix them in.

3 Knead the mixture with your hands until it becomes a smooth, thick paste. Add extra confectioners' sugar if the mixture is sticky.

CANDY DISPLAY

Marzipan colors

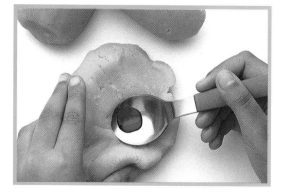

Split the marzipan into three balls. Leave one ball plain. Add a little pink coloring to one ball and green to the other. Knead until the color is even.

Roly-poly candies

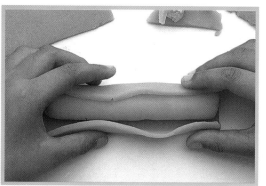

1 Roll some plain marzipan into a small log. Roll out the same amount of green and pink marzipan and cut each into a rectangle.

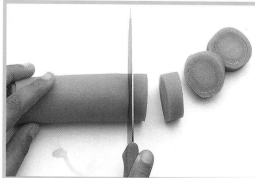

2 Roll the green and then the pink rectangles around the log. Then trim the ends and slice off small rounds to make the finished candies.

Checkerboard candies

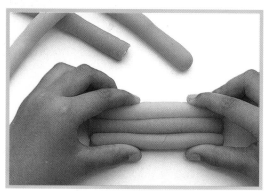

1 Cut six equal pieces of marzipan, two of each color. Roll them into long logs, then press three different-colored logs together.

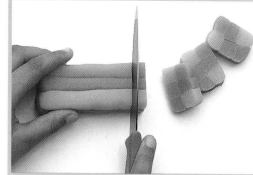

2 Press the remaining logs on top, making sure that no log is next to a log of the same color. Flatten the sides and cut into slices.

Cutout candies

Roll out some marzipan until it is about ¼ in. (0.5 cm) thick. Cut out shapes such as butterflies and flowers with the cookie cutters.

Sweet treats

Arrange the finished candies in a pretty pattern on a big plate or tray. Below is a guide to all the different types of candies.

Peppermint cream

Dark chocolate

Checked effect made with fork.

Pink sugar mouse

Currant eyes

Peanut ears

Licorice tail

Marzipan butterfly

Licorice body and antennae

Marzipan bauble

Checkerboard candy

Marzipan teardrop

Roly-poly candy

Marzipan flower

Three rings of colored marzipan

Candied cherry piece

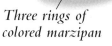

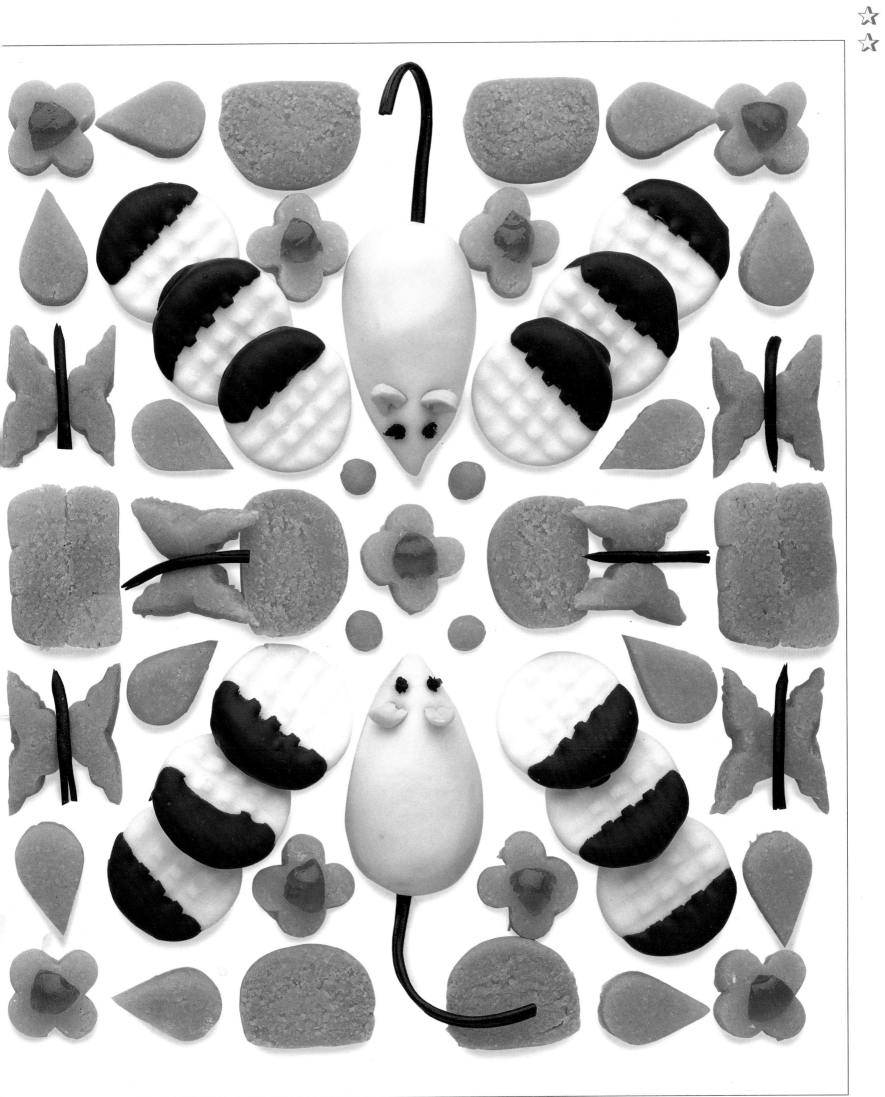

MUFFIN BONANZA

Muffins are quick to make and taste delicious still warm from the oven. Try one of the three versions shown here: white chocolate and strawberry, orange and poppy seed, or apple and cinnamon. Alternatively, you could add your own ingredients to the basic recipe. The quantity given here makes 12 muffins.

EQUIPMENT

Muffin tin

Cutting board

Wire cooling rack

Fork

Spoon

Sieve

Wooden spoon

Paper muffin cups

Mixing bowl

Small bowl

Small saucepan

Sharp knife

You will need

For the basic mixture

1 cup/8 fl oz /240 ml milk

6 tbs/3 oz/85 g soft brown sugar

2 eggs

1 level tablespoon baking powder

A big pinch of salt

4 tbs/2 oz/55 g butter

1¼ cups/10 oz /285 g all-purpose flour

For white chocolate-strawberry muffins

Several strawberries

2 oz/55 g white chocolate drops

For apple-cinnamon muffins

1 teaspoon ground cinnamon

1 apple (to be peeled)

For orange-poppy seed muffins

Juice and grated rind of an orange★

1 tablespoon poppy seeds

What to do

1 Put the paper cups in the muffin tin. Preheat the oven to 400°F/ 200°C/Gas Mark 6. Melt the butter in the saucepan, then let it cool slightly.

2 Sift the flour, baking powder, salt, sugar, and ground cinnamon (if using it) into the mixing bowl and stir everything together.

3 Beat the eggs in the small bowl. Pour in the milk (and orange juice if using it)★ and whisk it into the eggs. Then stir in the melted butter.

★Replace ½ cup/4 fl oz/120 ml of the milk with the grated rind and juice of an orange for the orange-poppy seed muffins.

4 Peel the apple and chop it (or the strawberries) into small pieces. Add it, with the rest of the ingredients and the egg mixture, to the bowl of flour.

5 Beat all the ingredients together, then spoon the mixture into the muffin cups. Put them into the oven to bake for about 25 to 30 minutes.

6 The muffins are cooked when they have risen and are firm and golden brown. Move them carefully onto a wire rack to cool.

Tempting treats

Muffins taste best eaten warm from the oven on the day they are made. However, if you have any left uneaten, put them in an airtight tin and keep it in a cool place or in the freezer. They will stay fresh for several days.

Apple-cinnamon muffin

Orange-poppy seed muffin

Strawberry-white chocolate muffin

Pretty doily

For a special occasion, decorate your plates with pretty paper doilies. Take a 12-in. (30-cm) square of greaseproof paper and fold it in half, twice. Then, using scissors, cut a rounded edge opposite the point. Cut small shapes in the paper to make a pattern. Unfold it to discover a delicate doily.

Pretty greaseproof paper doily

JUNK JEWELRY

You don't need gold and precious gems to make fabulous jewelry. You can create stunning necklaces, bracelets, and earrings with paper and a few colorful bits and pieces. Look around your home for buttons, beads, shiny candy wrappers, and ribbons, then add sequins and glitter for extra sparkle.

EQUIPMENT

Spatula

Scissors

Pencil

Thick and thin knitting needles

You will need

For rolled-paper jewelry

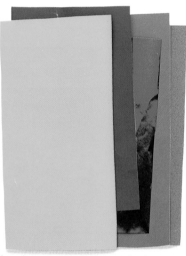

Colored paper in different thicknesses

Magazine pages

Narrow ribbons

For glitzy jewelry

Corrugated cardboard

Gold paper

Brightly colored sequins

Pin backs

Small, wooden beads

Glue stick

Glue in a tube

Clip-on earring backs

Scraps of colored foil and candy wrappers

Rolled-paper jewelry

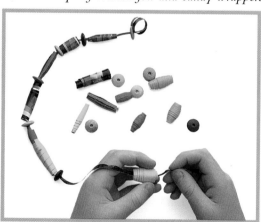

1 Cut out lots of long thin triangles from magazine pages and colored paper, as shown. The triangles should be about 12 in. (30 cm) long.

2 Spread glue on the thinnest two-thirds of each triangle. Then, starting with the wide end, roll each triangle around a knitting needle.

3 When you have enough paper beads, thread them onto some ribbon with a flat bead between each one. Tie the ribbon ends together.

Glitzy jewelry

1 Draw some shapes on corrugated cardboard and cut them out. Cut the same shapes out of gold paper and glue them onto the cardboard.

2 Tear up small pieces of colored foil and candy wrappers and glue them all over the gold shapes. Then glue sequins on top of the foil.

3 Make small holes in the gold shapes and thread them onto thin ribbons to make necklaces, or glue them onto earring or pin backs.

Colorful collection

Rainbow-bright and sparkling, the finished jewelry is great fun to wear and makes wonderful presents, too. Experiment with different shapes, designs, colors, and textures of paper.

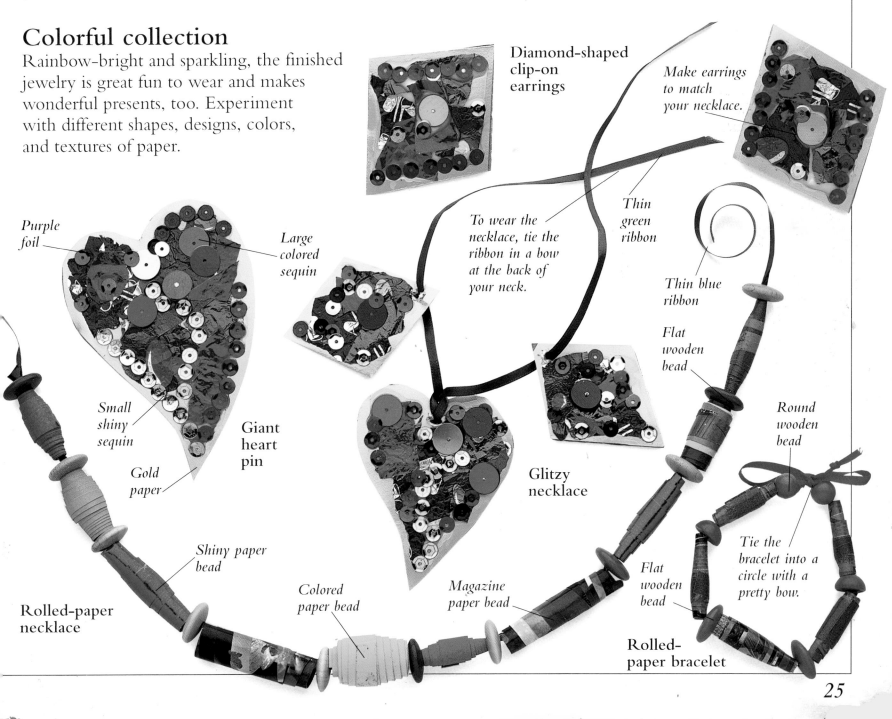

Diamond-shaped clip-on earrings

Make earrings to match your necklace.

To wear the necklace, tie the ribbon in a bow at the back of your neck.

Thin green ribbon

Thin blue ribbon

Flat wooden bead

Round wooden bead

Purple foil

Large colored sequin

Small shiny sequin

Gold paper

Giant heart pin

Glitzy necklace

Shiny paper bead

Rolled-paper necklace

Colored paper bead

Magazine paper bead

Flat wooden bead

Tie the bracelet into a circle with a pretty bow.

Rolled-paper bracelet

25

DOUGH MODELS

Salt dough is easy to make and can be modeled into all kinds of things. You can bake it in the oven so that it sets hard (ask an adult to help you) and then paint it bright colors. Here you can see how to make jazzy napkin rings, tiny pots, fabulous fishy key rings, and fun play-food pins.

Mixing bowl

Jar of water

Toothpicks

Baking sheet

Knife

Cooling rack

Thick and thin paintbrushes

You will need

³/₄ cup/¹/₃ pint /200 ml water

1 tablespoon vegetable oil

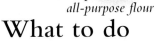

1¹/₄ cups/10 oz/300 g all-purpose flour

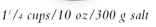

1¹/₄ cups/10 oz/300 g salt

Poster paints

Clear varnish

Key rings

Plastic clips

What to do

1 Set the oven to 350°F/180°C/Gas Mark 4. Mix the flour, salt, oil, and water into a soft dough in the bowl. Add more water if necessary.

2 Sprinkle some flour on a table. Turn the dough onto the table and knead it with your hands, as shown, until it is smooth and stretchy.

3 Then model the dough into the shapes you want. Stick pieces of dough together with a little water and use a toothpick to make small holes.

Fishy friends
You can use your models to make great presents, like fridge magnets, key rings, and note clips.

Fishy clip

4 Make a pot by coiling strips of dough around a circular base. Put all the dough shapes on a baking sheet and bake them for 20 minutes.

5 Let the dough shapes cool on a wire rack, then paint them in bright colors. When the paint has dried, coat them with clear varnish.

Glue a fish onto a small magnet.

Fridge magnet

Play cakes

Play meal

Jewel bright

Here are some of the many things you can make with salt dough. Once they are painted and varnished, they will last forever. Try making salt dough jewelry, too.

Tie a fish to a key ring with ribbon.

Key ring

Play fruit

Play-food pins
Tape your mini-plate to a safety pin to make a colorful jewelry pin.

Paint your pots with colorful designs.

Make a personalized napkin ring for each member of your family.

Tiny pots
You can keep beads, jewelry, and other treasures in these pretty pots.

Napkin rings
These colorful rings will brighten up any table. You could try making a bracelet in the same way.

ALL IN A POT

You can create a beautiful garden anywhere. Flowers, herbs, and even fruit can be grown indoors in pots and window boxes. Start planting today, and watch your own garden blossom to life in front of your eyes. Turn the page for lots of interesting mini-garden ideas.

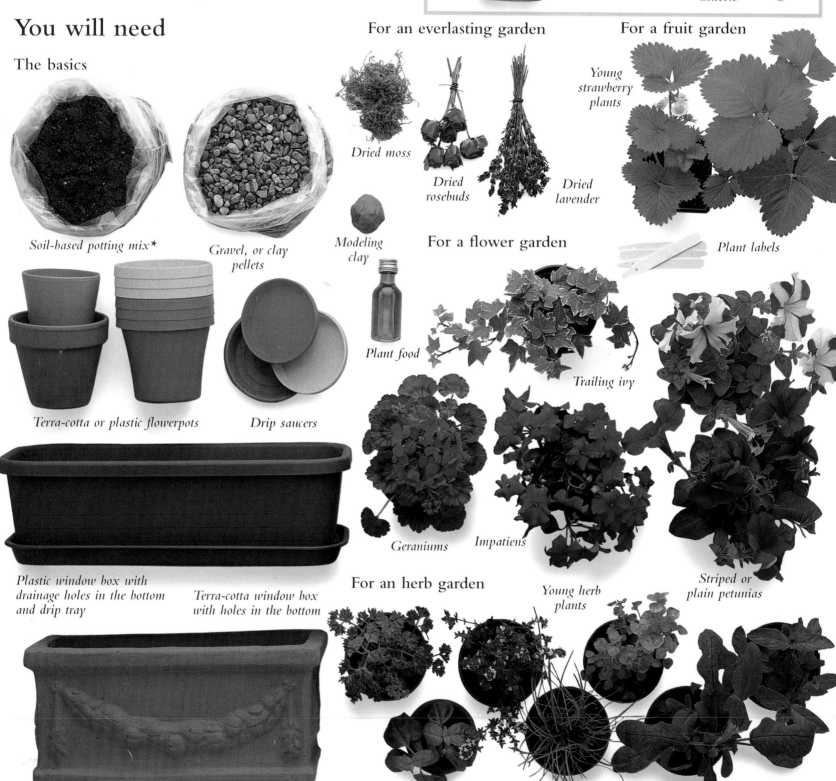

EQUIPMENT

Watering can

Spade

Scissors

You will need

The basics

Soil-based potting mix*

Gravel, or clay pellets

Terra-cotta or plastic flowerpots

Drip saucers

Plastic window box with drainage holes in the bottom and drip tray

Terra-cotta window box with holes in the bottom

For an everlasting garden

Dried moss

Dried rosebuds

Dried lavender

Modeling clay

Plant food

For a flower garden

Trailing ivy

Geraniums

Impatiens

For an herb garden

Young herb plants

For a fruit garden

Young strawberry plants

Plant labels

Striped or plain petunias

*It is much better to use potting soil than ordinary garden soil.

Preparing for planting

1 Fill the bottom of the window box and flowerpots with a layer of gravel. This will help water drain out of the pots.

2 Then half-fill the window box and pots with potting soil. If the soil is very dry, water it lightly before planting anything.

Repotting a plant

Lower the plant into the flowerpot so that the bottom of its stem is just below the pot rim. Fill in the sides with soil and press it down firmly.

A flower garden

1 Take the plants out of their pots and decide how to arrange them. Start with the tallest plants. They look good at the back of the box.

2 Then add any low, trailing plants. It is best to put these at the front, so that they can grow down over the window box.

3 Arrange the rest of your flowers in the box. Then fill in the gaps between them with more soil and press it down firmly.

An everlasting garden

1 Break off a piece of modeling clay and press it into the bottom of a small flowerpot. This will keep the stems of the dried flowers in place.

2 Trim the stems of the dried flowers. Then start arranging them in the flowerpot by pressing them gently into the modeling clay.

3 When all the dried flowers are in place, arrange a little dried moss around the top of the pot to make it look as if they are growing naturally.

GARDENS IN POTS

These pots and boxes of brightly colored flowering plants will cheer up any room or garden. Look for a sunny, sheltered spot to grow your plants, such as outside on a window ledge or inside on a wide shelf or windowsill. A window box is very heavy, so you will need to ask an adult to move it.

Lavender and rose garden

Dried rose garden

Lavender garden

Terra-cotta flowerpot

Dried rose

Dried lavender

Moss

Everlasting flowers

These pretty dried flower gardens will never die. But they should be kept out of direct sunlight or their colors will soon fade.

Red geranium

Ivy

Marjoram

These ivy plants have green-and-white leaves.

Yellow plastic pot

One plant to a pot

If you don't have a window box, why not plant a group of plants in matching pots? Stand them in a row for a striking effect.

Painted pots

Try growing house plants in brightly painted pots. You can find out how to decorate flowerpots and drip saucers on page 32.

This white flower will soon lose its petals, then its middle will swell and redden to form a strawberry.

Strawberry plants

Tiny unripe strawberry

Red petunia

Strawberry garden

Early in the summer, these strawberry plants are still flowering. If you look closely, you can see small green strawberries forming. Before long, the strawberries will grow and ripen. They are ready to pick when the berries have turned red.

Trailing ivy plant

Green plastic window box and drip saucer

White plastic window box and drip tray

Herb garden

Fresh herbs look pretty sitting on a kitchen windowsill and they make the kitchen smell delicious, too. It is best to trim them often, to keep the plants from becoming too big. If you grow herbs outside, their flowers will attract bees and butterflies.

Chives

Golden marjoram

Purple sage

Parsley

Growing mint
Mint spreads quickly, so it is a good idea to grow it in its own pot.

Mint

Summer garden

This colorful window box will flower all through the summer. It will need watering once a day, or more often on hot days. Removing dead flowers will make the plant flower for longer.

Terra-cotta pot with drip saucer

Thyme

Pretty terra-cotta window box

Caring for your plants

Red geranium

Red-and-white striped petunias

Purple petunia

1 Your pots and window boxes will need watering every day in warm weather. The soil should always feel slightly moist.

Scarlet impatiens

2 All plants will flower for longer and look better if you deadhead them regularly. This means snipping or picking off any dead flowers.

PERFECT POTS

Why not add color to a collection of plants by painting some flowerpots? You can make a single-color pot, add stripes or checks, or even paint on some flowers. For the best effects, keep the paint fairly thick and the patterns simple. Your painted pots will make wonderful presents.

EQUIPMENT

Fine paintbrush

Thick paintbrush

Saucer

Jar of water

You will need

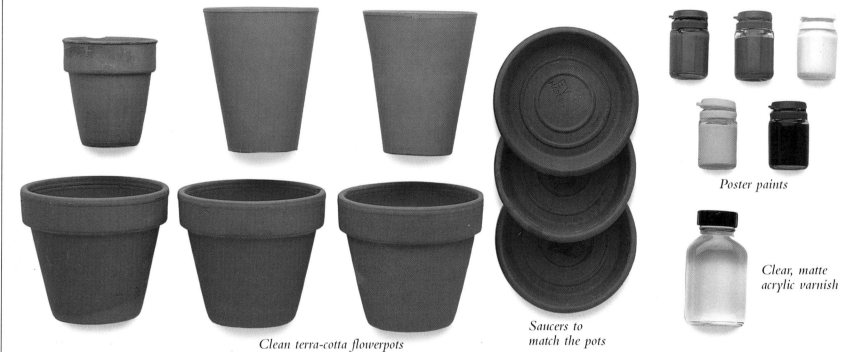

Poster paints

Clear, matte acrylic varnish

Clean terra-cotta flowerpots

Saucers to match the pots

What to do

1 First mix the colors you want on a saucer. Use a thick brush to paint plain pots one color at a time. You can paint flowers straight onto a pot.

2 To make patterns, paint pots in one color and leave them to dry. Then paint stripes or checks in other colors on top of the first color.

3 When the paint has dried, brush on a coat of clear varnish. This will make the pots waterproof and keep the paint from running.

Plenty of pots

You can add a finishing touch to your pots by painting matching patterns around the rims. Use the decorated pots to hold anything from your favorite plants or some candles, to a collection of colored pencils.

Paint crisscross lines for a plaid design.

A colorful row of flowers around the side of a pot will brighten up a green houseplant.

If the pot has a matching saucer, paint a pattern on the side of it to match the pot.

PRESSING PLANTS

Pressed flowers and leaves are beautiful and they last forever. Flowers with flat faces are the easiest to press. Choose dry, undamaged flowers and leaves, and press them as quickly as you can, before they start to droop. You can stick them in a nature diary or use them to make pictures and cards. Below you can find out how to press plants. Turn the page to see more ideas for things to make.

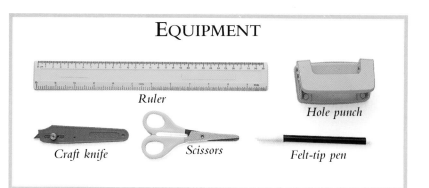

EQUIPMENT

Ruler

Hole punch

Craft knife

Scissors

Felt-tip pen

You will need

Fresh flowers and leaves to press

A heavy book

Geranium

Pansies

Ivy leaves

Bellflower

Daisies

Columbine

Fern

Welsh Poppy

Rose

Purple sage

Buttercup

Blotting paper

Violas

Parsley

For making pictures

Rubber cement

Cotton swabs

For the nature diary

Corrugated cardboard

Different sorts of paper

Tracing paper

Thin ribbon

Clear adhesive plastic

Thick paper

Pressing flowers

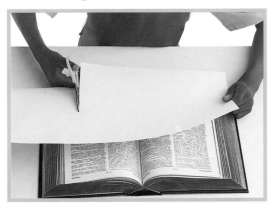

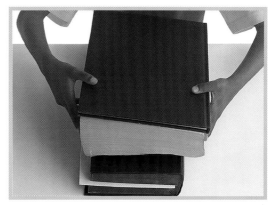

1 Open the heavy book and cut a piece of blotting paper about the same size as the open pages. Crease the paper in half, then lay it on the book.

2 Arrange flowers and leaves flat on the right-hand side of the paper, then fold the left-hand side over, and close the book.

3 Press more flowers throughout the book. Stack heavy books on top. Leave the plants to dry for at least four weeks.

Making a nature diary

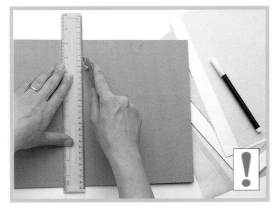

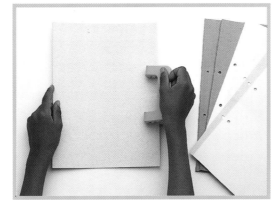

1 Decide what size you want your diary to be. Then ask an adult to cut two pieces of corrugated cardboard to make the front and back covers.

2 Cut out rectangles of paper and tracing paper just smaller than the covers to make pages. Punch holes in both the pages and covers, as shown.

3 Put the paper and tracing paper inside the two covers, with the holes lined up★. Tie ribbons through the holes to hold the book together.

Making pictures

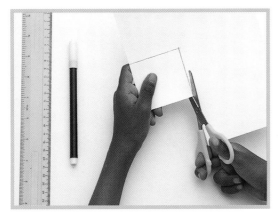

1 Cut out different-shaped pieces of white or colored thick paper. These will be the bases for your cards, pictures, gift tags, and bookmarks.

2 Arrange flowers and leaves on the paper. Dab a tiny spot of rubber cement on the back of each flower and leaf and then stick them in position.

3 To protect your picture, cut a piece of adhesive plastic just bigger than you need. Smooth it onto the picture and fold the edges over the back.

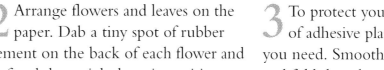

Alternate pages of tracing paper and paper inside the covers. Tie ribbons through all the holes.

NATURE ON PAPER

Pressing plants is a wonderful way of keeping a picture record of all the plants you have seen – on vacation, in the park, and in your own yard. Along with flowers, you can press leaves, ferns, mosses, seed heads, and herbs.* Keep them in a nature diary or arrange them into pictures.

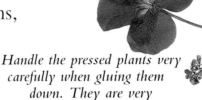

Handle the pressed plants very carefully when gluing them down. They are very fragile.

Flowers and leaves May

Herbal diary
You could use some pages in your diary to collect and label one type of plant, such as herbs.

Tracing paper sheet

Nature diary
Your nature diary can be a picture record of the changing seasons, with every couple of pages displaying the plants you collect each month. Even in winter you will be able to find interesting things for your diary. Put a page of tracing paper between each page of plants to keep them from sticking together.

Remember – never pick or uproot wild plants.

Flower picture
Arrange pressed flowers on a piece of paper, then mount the paper on a piece of cardboard or thick paper. Tape a loop of ribbon to the back and hang it up. You can arrange the flowers in patterns or try to make a picture with your pressed flowers and leaves.

Bookmark
Use narrow strips of thick paper to make bookmarks and protect the designs with adhesive plastic.

Nature diary's corrugated cardboard cover

Gray paper mount

Thread ribbons through a slit in the cover for tying the nature diary shut.

Yellow ribbon tie

Cover the tag with adhesive plastic.

Gift tags
Glue pressed flowers or leaves to a square of paper. Then punch a hole in one corner of each tag and tie a ribbon through it.

NATURE'S MODELS

When you go out for a walk at home or on vacation, keep your eyes open for interesting objects such as oddly shaped pieces of driftwood and sticks, unusual pebbles, shells, leaves, seeds, and other bits and pieces. With a little imagination, you can transform them into all kinds of models and toys. Here you can find ideas for making funny faces, wriggly snakes, boats, and a little cart. Turn the page to see what they look like.

You will need

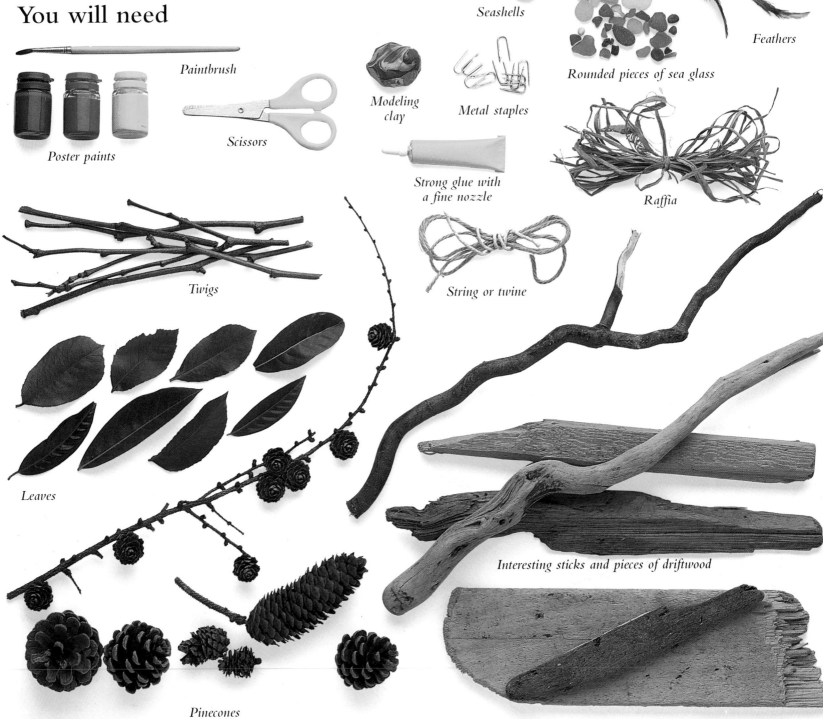

Seashells

Feathers

Paintbrush

Rounded pieces of sea glass

Poster paints

Scissors

Modeling clay

Metal staples

Strong glue with a fine nozzle

Raffia

Twigs

String or twine

Leaves

Interesting sticks and pieces of driftwood

Pinecones

Funny face

Find a flat piece of wood for the face and glue small stones, cones, or shells to it to make the features. You could use feathers or string for the hair.

Wriggly snake

Find a twisted stick and ask an adult to smooth out any rough spots. Then paint on a face and some stripes to make a snake's skin.

Seashell sailboats

Stick small pieces of modeling clay into some shells. Thread leaves onto small sticks for the sails and push them into the modeling clay.

Jaunty clipper

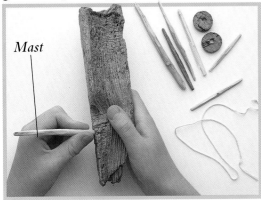

Mast

Rigging   Cork ring   Yardarm

Mast

Bowsprit

Bundle of twigs tied up with raffia

1 Ask an adult to make holes in the top of a flat piece of wood. Put sticks in the holes, for masts. Add a feather shaft to make the bowsprit.

2 Tie small sticks to the masts to make yardarms. Glue a ring of cork to the top of each mast. Tie string to the masts for the rigging.

One end of the string is tied to a short stick.

Caveman's cart   *Stick axle*

Axle

1 To make wheels, ask an adult to saw four slices of wood from a branch and drill a hole in the middle of each. Glue them onto the ends of two sticks.

2 Find a flat rectangle of wood. Ask an adult to drill a hole in one end. Carefully nail the two axles to the wood with metal staples, as shown.

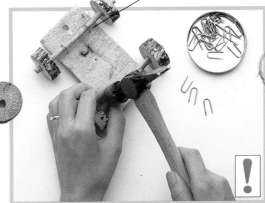

3 Cut a length of string. Tie one end to a small stick and the other to the cart. Then tie up a bundle of twigs and put it on the cart.

BEACHCOMBER'S GALLERY

Funny faces
These two faces are both stuck onto pieces of driftwood. Try out different objects for the features before gluing anything down.

And here are the finished models, together with another face! Use them as a starting point for your ideas and design your own models. What you make will vary, depending on the natural materials you have at home.

Paper hat decorated with a feather and a twisted stick

Sea glass eyes

Shell nose

Shells for earrings

Leaf mouth

Dancing lady

Shell necklace

Thick stick for arms

Feather headdress

Pinecone eyes

Pebble nose

Mouth made from an old piece of cork

King of the forest

Wriggly snakes
Use two or three paint colors for each twisting stick snake and try to keep the pattern regular. Look at pictures of real snakes for inspiration. Paint on eyes and a mouth to add the finishing touches.

Caveman's load made from a collection of twigs

Sail made from a leaf

Twig mast

Wooden base

Seashell sailboats
Load your sailboats with a bounty of sea glass and see how well they float.

Stick axle

Slices of round branch for wheels

Shell boat

Treasure of sea glass and tiny shells

This snake has a smiling face.

String for pulling the cart along

Sails and flags made from scraps of paper

Cork circle crow's nest

Caveman's cart
You can use your cart to display some of your nature treasures. Then you could make little people out of sticks and string to pull the cart along.

Rigging made from fine string

You can vary the number of masts and sails you make to suit the piece of wood.

Yardarm made from a short stick

Jaunty clipper
This driftwood boat would look good on display in your room.

Feather shaft for a bowsprit

Fine string joints

Yellow-and-green pattern

Old piece of rope for waves

41

SPINNING WINDMILLS

Try making these colorful paper windmills. Big windmills catch the wind in their sails to grind grain into flour, to pump water, and even to produce electricity, but these little windmills are just for fun. See how fast you can make them spin by blowing on their sails. When the weather is nice, take them outside to spin around in the wind.

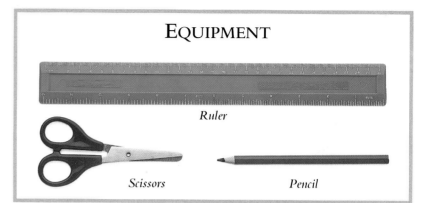

EQUIPMENT

Ruler

Scissors

Pencil

You will need

Pins with large heads

Small beads

Pencils with erasers on the ends

Sheets of colored paper

What to do

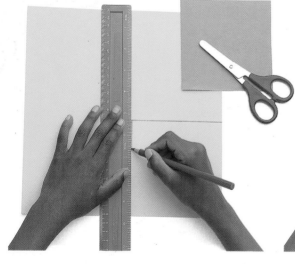

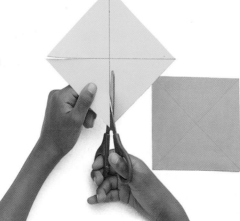

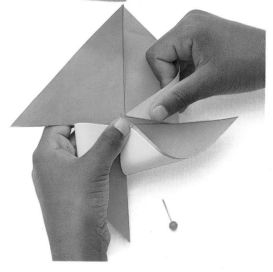

1 Using the ruler, measure out and draw two equal-size squares on two different-colored pieces of paper (see page 60). Cut out the squares.

2 Using the ruler again, draw two diagonal lines across each square so they cross in the middle. Cut only two-thirds of the way along each line.

3 Hold the squares of paper together. Bend the paper back along each cut line into the center as shown, and hold the corners down.

42

Make sure the sharp end of the pin doesn't stick out of the eraser.

Bead

Big windmill with red-and-yellow sails

Blue pin

4 Push a pin through all the corners of paper, then through a bead and into the eraser at the end of a pencil.

Red pin

Rainbow pencil handle

Blue-and-yellow sails

5 Blow on the windmill to make it spin. Does it work best if you blow from the side or the front?

Green-and-yellow sails

Green pin

Test of strength
Use a windmill to test how windy it is. The faster the sails of your windmill turn, the stronger the wind is.

Host of windmills

Here are all the finished windmills. You can make windmills with bigger or smaller sails by using different-sized squares of paper. If the paper is very thick, you will only need one square of paper.

Orange pencil handle

FINGER PUPPETS

You can design a cheerful handful of finger puppets using the template shown on page 62. Make the puppets from brightly colored felt, or from any scraps of fabric or paper you can find at home. Try the animal puppets shown here, or invent some of your own.

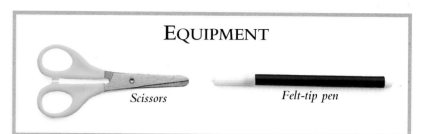

EQUIPMENT

Scissors

Felt-tip pen

You will need

Template (see page 62)

Brightly colored felt, fabric scraps, or paper

Strong glue in a tube with a fine nozzle

Pieces of paper, for designing your puppets

What to do

1 Draw the designs for your puppets on paper before you make them. Look at pictures of animals or people to get some ideas, then simplify them.

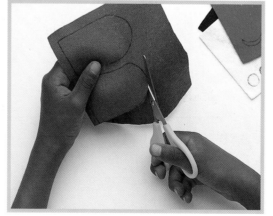

2 Lay the body template on a piece of felt and draw around it twice. Draw the puppet features on other pieces of felt. Cut out the body pieces.

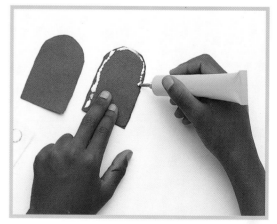

3 Spread a fine line of glue around the curved edge of one piece of the body, leaving the bottom edge free. Press the two body pieces together.

Cheerful puppets

You could make a whole group of smiling animals like these, or a collection of characters from fairy tales. Your puppets will work best if they are simple and brightly colored. Why not make up a play for the puppets with a friend?

Put the puppets on your index finger.

4 Now carefully cut out the puppet features that you drew on the other pieces of felt. Remember to cut out two arms, two legs, etc.

5 Arrange the cutout features on the body to see how they look. If any part doesn't look quite right, try making another version of it.

6 First glue the legs and arms (or wings or paws) to the base of the body. Then glue the rest of the animal's features onto the front.

Mouse

Owl

Lion

Panda

Rooster

Frog

Parrot

Pig

Moving the puppets

Make the puppets look as though they are talking by moving your finger.

KALEIDOSCOPE

A kaleidoscope is a very clever toy – hold it to your eye, turn it around, and watch an unending display of patterns. You can make one yourself from shiny mirror board★ or from aluminum foil glued onto cardboard. The kaleidoscope works best if your colored pieces are thicker than ordinary paper.

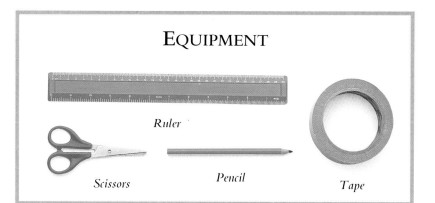

EQUIPMENT

Ruler

Scissors *Pencil* *Tape*

You will need

Mirror board

Transparent beads, small pieces of colored acetate or plastic

Clear plastic (from a bag)

Tracing paper

Colored paper

Glue stick

White cardboard

What to do

1 Cut out a piece of mirror board 4½ in. (12 cm) by 8 in. (20 cm). Measure out and score two lines along it lengthways 1½ in. (4 cm) apart.
★You can buy this at arts and crafts stores.

2 Fold the board along the lines, so the mirror is inside. Tape the two edges together. Then tape a piece of clear plastic over one end of the tube.

3 Cut another piece of mirror board 5 in. (12.5 cm) by 1¼ in. (3 cm). Tape it around the tube, so that it sticks out over the covered end, as shown.

What to do (continued)

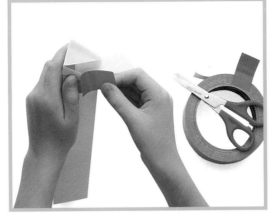

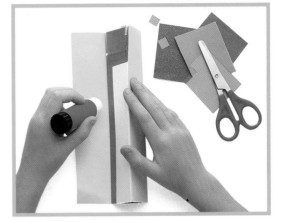

4 Hold the tube upright with the short piece of tube you have added at the top. Drop small pieces of colored plastic and beads into it.

5 Cut out a triangular piece of tracing paper. Lay it flat over the top of the tube. Fold the edges over the tube and tape them down.

6 Cut out a piece of colored paper 5 in. (12.5 cm) by 8 in. (20 cm). Glue it around the tube, as shown, then decorate it with paper shapes.

Pocket rainbows

Here is the finished kaleidoscope, decorated with colorful paper rectangles and squares. To make it work, face a window or another bright light and close one eye. Hold the open end of the tube up to your other eye, look into the tube, and slowly turn the kaleidoscope around. On the right are some of the patterns we saw.

As you turn the kaleidoscope around in your hands, the pattern will change before your eyes.

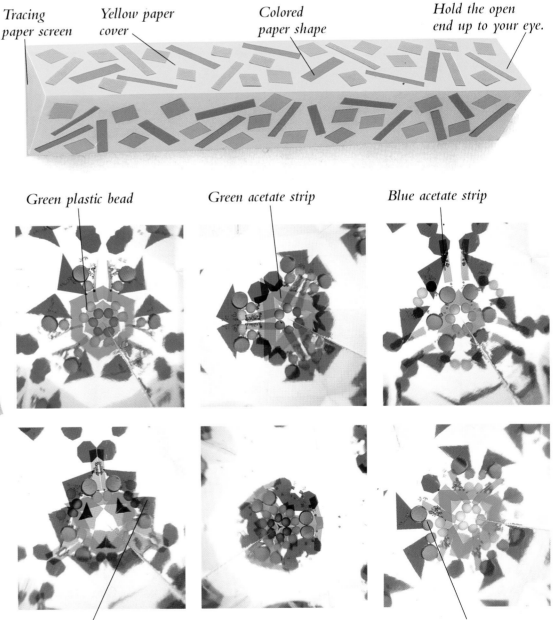

Tracing paper screen *Yellow paper cover* *Colored paper shape* *Hold the open end up to your eye.*

Green plastic bead *Green acetate strip* *Blue acetate strip*

Red acetate triangle *Blue plastic bead*

JUNK MODELS

You do not need expensive materials or kits to make exciting models. Here you can learn how to make toy binoculars, a truck, a robot, and an impressive castle – all from everyday materials that you would normally just throw away. Turn the page to find out how to put the finishing touches on the models.

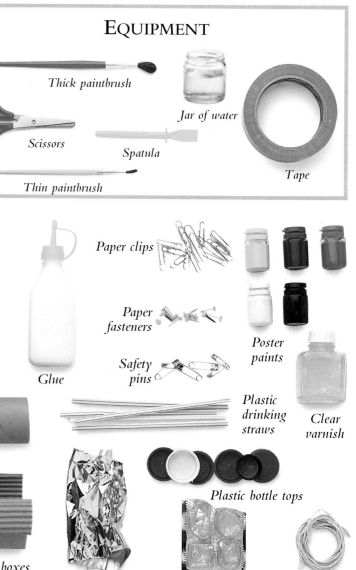

EQUIPMENT

Thick paintbrush

Jar of water

Scissors

Spatula

Tape

Thin paintbrush

You will need

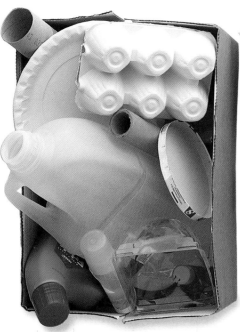

Any empty cartons, tubes, and packages

Cardboard boxes

Cardboard toilet-paper roll tubes

Glue

Long cardboard tubes

Corrugated cardboard from old boxes

Paper clips

Paper fasteners

Safety pins

Poster paints

Plastic drinking straws

Clear varnish

Old aluminum foil

Plastic candy containers

Plastic bottle tops

String

Making binoculars

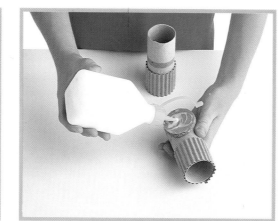

1 Cut two corrugated cardboard strips 2 in. (5 cm) wide and long enough to wrap around a small tube. Glue one around the end of each tube.

2 Draw around a tube four times on corrugated cardboard and cut out the four circles. Glue them together between the two tubes, as shown.

3 Ask an adult to make a hole in each tube. Thread a piece of string through the holes, and tie a knot in each end, as shown.

Making a truck

1 Find two boxes and a lid like these. Draw windows on the front and sides of the larger box and cut them out. This will be the cab of the truck.

2 Glue the box lid and the two boxes together on top of a piece of cardboard. Glue small tubes underneath the truck for the wheels.

3 Push plastic bottle tops into the ends of the tubes to complete the wheels. Then paint the truck with brightly colored poster paints.

Making a castle

1 Find a large box for the base of the castle. Cut four strips of cardboard, each the same length as a side of the box. Cut battlements in them.

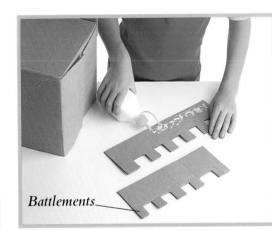

Battlements

2 Spread glue along the base of each strip of battlements and glue them around the base of the box, as shown, so the battlements stick up.

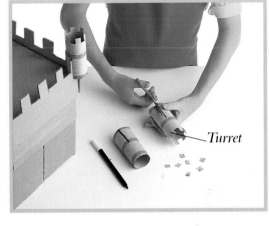

Turret

3 For turrets, cut battlements at the tops of four small tubes. Cut two slits in the bottom of each tube. Slot them onto the corners of the castle.

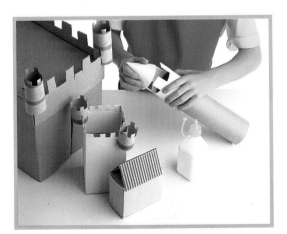

4 Use a long tube for a tall tower. Cut battlements in a strip of paper and glue it around the top. Then glue on a cone of paper for the roof.

5 Make small buildings for the castle from smaller boxes. Use corrugated cardboard to make roofs, windows, and doors. Then paint the buildings.

6 Glue all the bits of the castle together. Paint it, adding narrow windows. Make flags from folded paper triangles and tape them to straws.

CARDBOARD CREATIONS

Making a robot

Here are some of the models you can create. The truck and binoculars only take about an hour to make. The robot takes slightly longer, and the castle at least an afternoon. The models you make will look different, depending on the boxes and bits of junk you use. Have fun experimenting!

1 Attach small tube arms to a box body with paper fasteners. Ask an adult to make holes in the tubes and box, then push the fasteners through and open them.

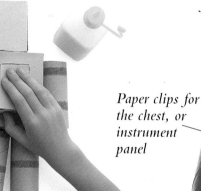

2 Glue the rest of the boxes together as shown. Use two small tubes for the legs, and small boxes for the head, feet, and chest.

3 Paint the robot and leave it to dry. Then coat it with clear varnish. When the varnish is dry, add details for the face, hands, uniform, and chest.

Plastic lid for a hat

Candy container for a mask

Small box for the head

Pieces of egg carton covered in foil for ears

Safety pin mouth

Foil-covered bottle tops for epaulets

Paper clips for the chest, or instrument panel

Small cardboard tube arm

Foil-covered bottle top for a hand

Gold tacks for buttons

Robot captain
The basic robot is made of one large box and four smaller boxes, with cardboard tubes for arms and legs. Paint your robot a bright color, then add shiny details with paper clips, tacks, and foil-covered bottle tops.

Sturdy cardboard tube legs

Small boxes for feet

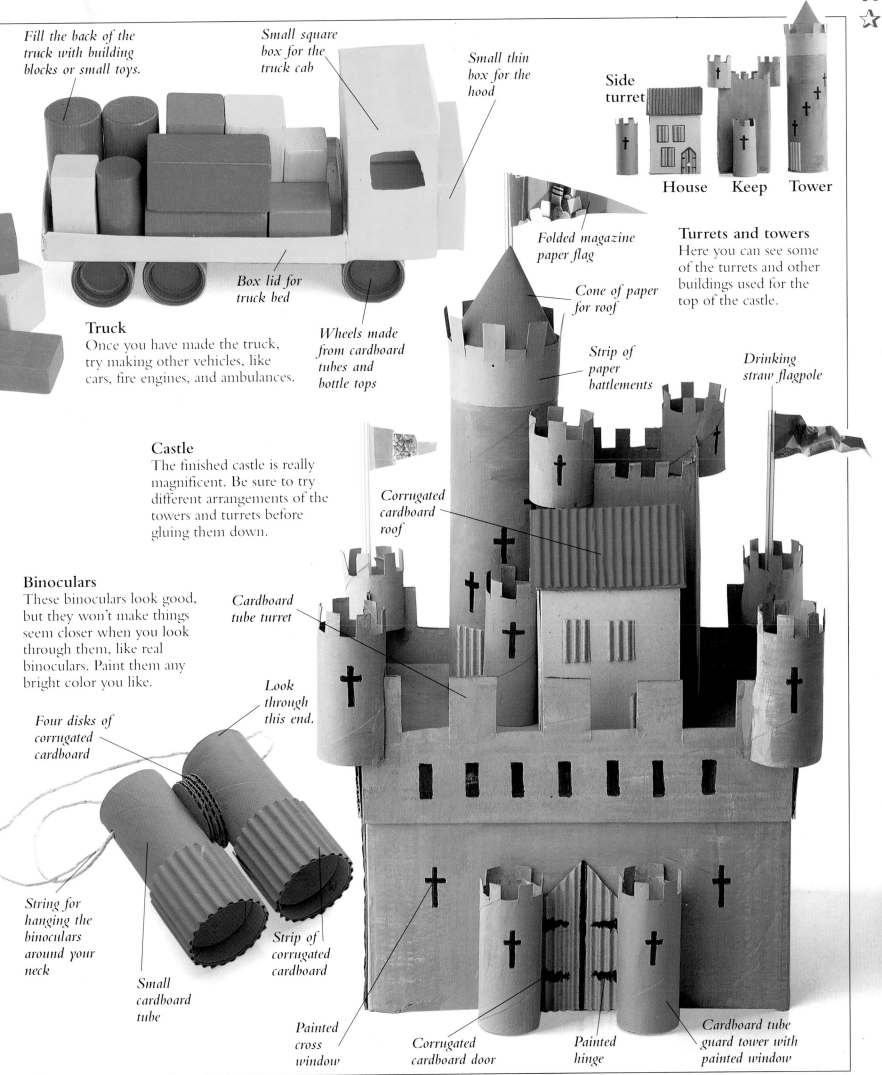

Fill the back of the truck with building blocks or small toys.

Small square box for the truck cab

Small thin box for the hood

Side turret

House   Keep   Tower

Turrets and towers
Here you can see some of the turrets and other buildings used for the top of the castle.

Folded magazine paper flag

Cone of paper for roof

Truck
Once you have made the truck, try making other vehicles, like cars, fire engines, and ambulances.

Box lid for truck bed

Wheels made from cardboard tubes and bottle tops

Strip of paper battlements

Drinking straw flagpole

Castle
The finished castle is really magnificent. Be sure to try different arrangements of the towers and turrets before gluing them down.

Corrugated cardboard roof

Binoculars
These binoculars look good, but they won't make things seem closer when you look through them, like real binoculars. Paint them any bright color you like.

Cardboard tube turret

Four disks of corrugated cardboard

Look through this end.

String for hanging the binoculars around your neck

Small cardboard tube

Strip of corrugated cardboard

Painted cross window

Corrugated cardboard door

Painted hinge

Cardboard tube guard tower with painted window

SHADOW PUPPETS

Putting on a shadow play with your friends is a great way to spend a rainy afternoon. Here you can find out how to make brightly colored shadow puppets with moving joints. Turn the page to see how to make the shadow theater and to find out how to work the puppets and put on a show.

You will need

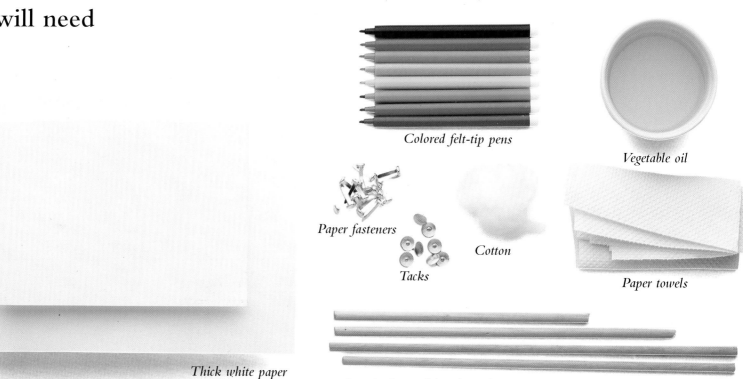

Colored felt-tip pens

Vegetable oil

Paper fasteners

Cotton

Tacks

Paper towels

Thick white paper

2 or 3 pieces of doweling about 12 in. (30 cm) long for each puppet

Making a puppet

1 Draw the puppet you want to make on white paper with a black felt-tip pen. Keep the shape simple but add details such as stripes and spots.

2 Color in the puppet with felt-tip pens. The brighter the colors, the better the puppet will look in the theater. Then cut it out carefully.

3 Next, cut off any part of the puppet that you want to be able to move. This puppet will have a neck that can move up and down.

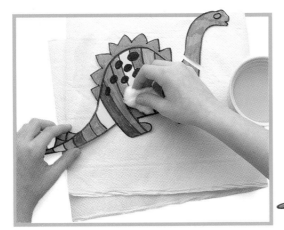

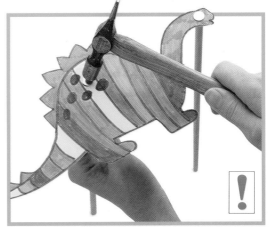

4 Lay the puppet on some paper towels and rub it all over with cotton soaked in vegetable oil. Do this to both sides of each puppet.

5 Make holes with a tack in the parts of the puppet you want to join. Push a paper fastener through each hole, and fold its legs open.

6 Then ask an adult to join a dowel rod to both parts of the puppet by hammering a tack into the end of a rod, as shown.

Puppet world

Here are some ideas for shadow puppets and scenery for the theater. Copy these, or make puppets of characters from your favorite stories.

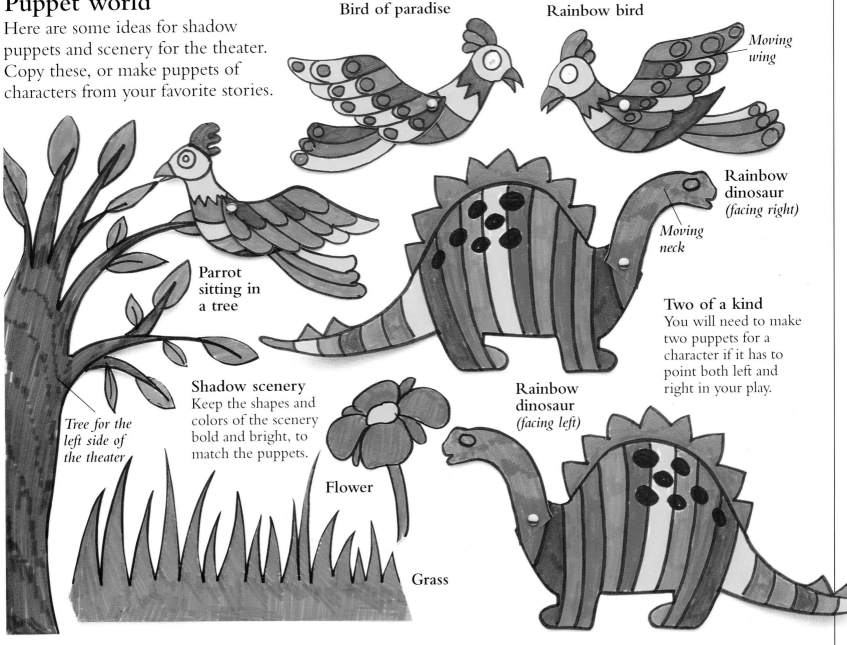

Bird of paradise

Rainbow bird

Moving wing

Parrot sitting in a tree

Rainbow dinosaur *(facing right)*

Moving neck

Two of a kind
You will need to make two puppets for a character if it has to point both left and right in your play.

Tree for the left side of the theater

Shadow scenery
Keep the shapes and colors of the scenery bold and bright, to match the puppets.

Flower

Rainbow dinosaur *(facing left)*

Grass

WORLD IN A THEATER

To bring the puppets to life, stand the theater on a table near a bright light, angled so that light shines in through the back of the box and onto the puppets and the screen. Make up a simple story script, and then you are ready to rehearse. You will need to ask a friend to help you because two hands are needed to work each puppet.

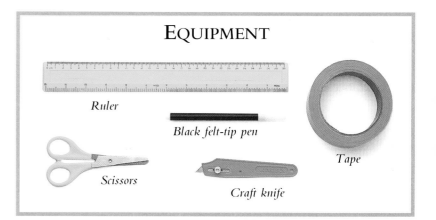

EQUIPMENT

Ruler

Black felt-tip pen

Scissors

Craft knife

Tape

You will need

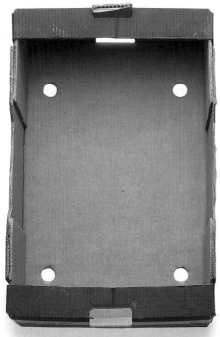

A strong, rectangular cardboard box

Colored paper for decorating the theater

Glue stick *Tracing paper*

Making the theater

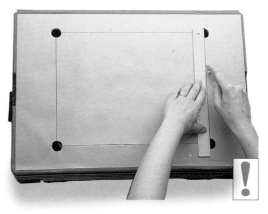

1 Measure and draw a rectangle on the bottom of the cardboard box, as shown. Then ask an adult to cut it out of the box with a craft knife.

!

2 Cut out a rectangle of tracing paper slightly bigger than the hole in the box. Tape the edges of the paper around the hole, inside the box.

3 Tape the pieces of scenery you have made, such as trees, flowers, and grass, colored-side down onto the paper screen inside the box.

4 Turn the box over. Cut out shapes from colored paper and glue them around the edge of the screen to make the box look like a real theater.

Make the bird fly by moving its wing up and down.

Hold one puppet stick in each hand.

Slide the puppet across the screen as you move its wing.

Behind the scenes
When you are ready to perform your play, stand to one side, behind the screen.

Move your arm up and down to move the dinosaur's head.

Moving puppets
You will need both hands to make each puppet move, one for each stick. To bring a puppet to life, slide it along the back of the screen while moving the sticks.

Be careful not to block out the light from your light source.

Decorate the front of the theater with colorful paper shapes.

Rainbow dinosaur

Tape the scenery to the sides of the theater.

RAGGY DOLLS

Here, and on the next page, are some wonderful things to sew – little cats and bears, pretty hearts, a rag doll, and a rabbit. You can make all of them using leftover pieces of fabric you have at home. The templates are on pages 62-63 and directions for the sewing stitches are on page 61.

You will need

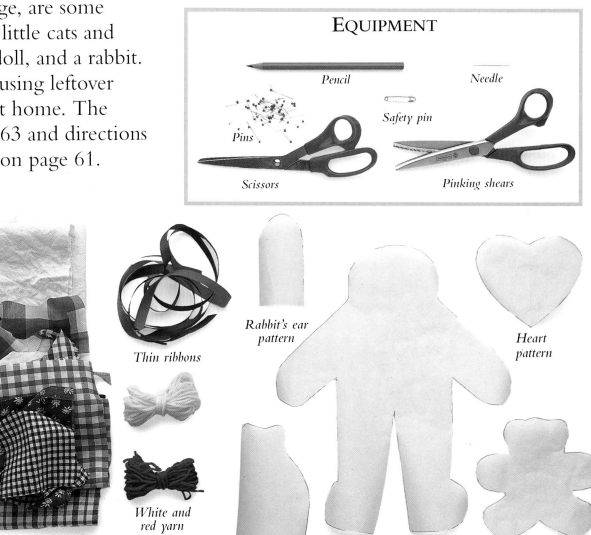

EQUIPMENT

Pencil

Needle

Pins

Safety pin

Scissors

Pinking shears

Soft stuffing

Spools of thread

Pieces of calico and gingham or other scraps of fabric

Thin ribbons

White and red yarn

Rabbit's ear pattern

Heart pattern

Cat pattern

Rabbit or doll pattern

Teddy pattern

(See pages 62-63 for all the templates)

Making the toys

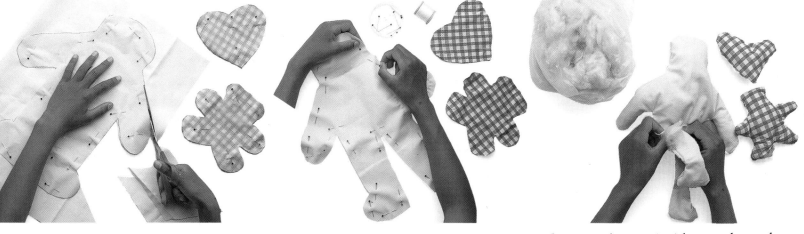

1 Fold some fabric in half. Pin the pattern to the folded fabric and cut it out, as shown, to give you two pieces. Then unpin the pattern.

2 Lay the two pieces of fabric right sides together. Pin and then sew★ them together, leaving a gap 2 in. (5 cm) wide at the end of the seam.

3 Turn the toy inside out through the 2-in. (5-cm) gap. Use a pencil to push out any narrow points. Then push some stuffing into the toy.

★ *Use running stitch for all seams, as shown on page 61.*

Finishing the rabbit

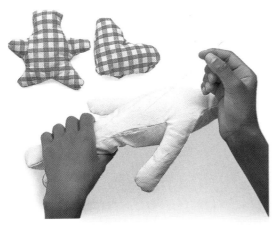

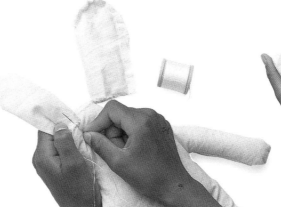

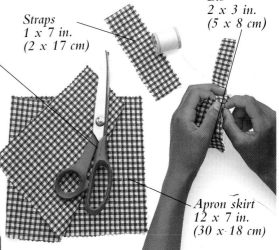

4 Use a pencil to push stuffing into any small corners. When the toy seems fat enough, sew up the gap in the seam using whipstitch.

1 Fold the rabbit ears in half and sew★ around the outer edges. Turn them inside out. Sew them to the top of the rabbit's head using whipstitch.

2 Sew eyes, a nose, a mouth, and whiskers on the rabbit's face using backstitch. Cut a strip of fabric and tie it on like a bow tie.

Finishing the doll

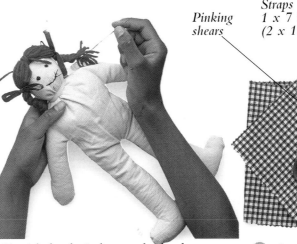

Long strands of red yarn

White yarn

Pinking shears

Straps 1 x 7 in. (2 x 17 cm)

Bib 2 x 3 in. (5 x 8 cm)

Apron skirt 12 x 7 in. (30 x 18 cm)

1 Tie white yarn around the doll's neck. Sew red yarn to her head for hair. Sew two ribbons to her face. Tie them in bows around her hair.

2 Braid the hair beneath the bows and tie each braid with red yarn. Then sew two eyes and a mouth on the doll's face using backstitch.

3 Cut out the apron pieces with shears. Fold the straps in half and whipstitch them to the bib. Put the bib on the doll so the straps cross at the back.

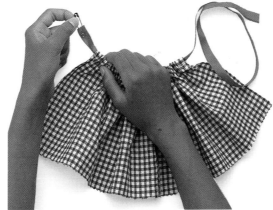

Trim off the ends of the ribbon.

Tie the apron around the doll.

4 Cut a 12-in. (30-cm) piece of ribbon. Fold the top of the apron over ¹/₂ in. (1 cm) and pin it down. Sew★ along the cut edge to make a loop.

5 Fasten a safety pin to one end of the ribbon and thread the ribbon through the loop. Then gather the skirt evenly along the ribbon.

DOLLS AND BEARS

Add bows and ribbons to your toys to give them a finishing touch. You can make them in matching fabrics as we have done here, or use any scraps you find at home. All of them would make good presents.

Dancing bears
Make three little bears. Tie bows around their necks and stitch them together at the paws. Sew ribbons on the free paws at each end of the row. These make an ideal present for a new baby's crib.

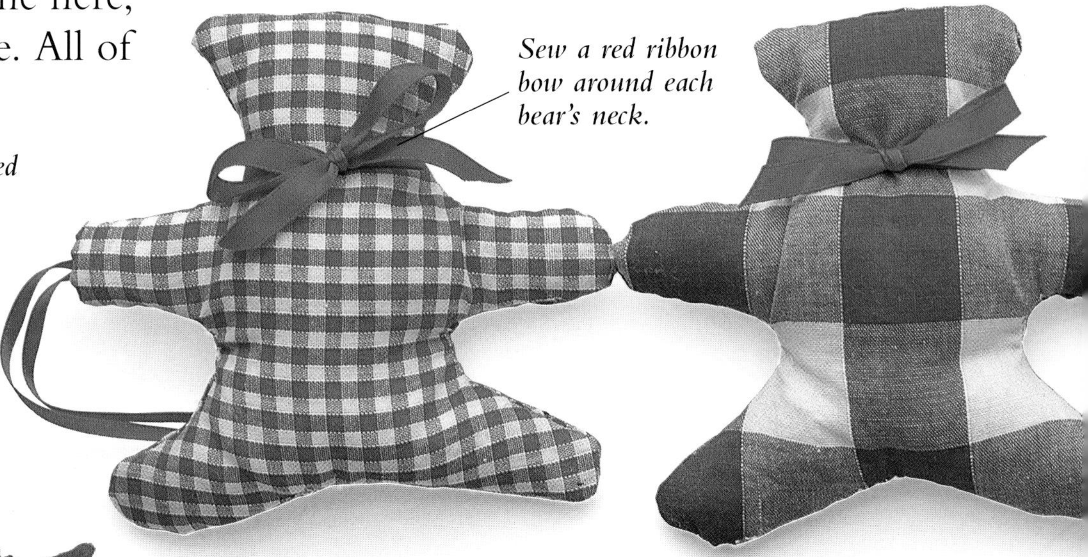

Red yarn hair made into braids

Embroidered face

Blue ribbon bow

Sew a red ribbon bow around each bear's neck.

Gingham apron

Blue ribbon bow

Martha doll
Martha is made of white calico and has a checked apron.

Soft hearts cushion
Make four stuffed hearts in different fabrics that go well together. Sew them together to make a flower shape and stitch a bow in the center.

Red-striped
fabric

Ribbons for tying
up the bears

Broad ribbon
loop for hanging
up the hearts

Embroidered
face and
whiskers

Gingham
bow tie

Red bow of
thin ribbon

White rabbit
The rabbit is made from the
same pattern as Martha
Doll, only he has floppy
ears as well. Tie a
jaunty bow tie around
his neck. Make him
a bouquet of dried
flowers and sew
them on the
inside of
one paw.

Tie a bow
around the
cat's neck to
give it a little
more shape.

Little cat
Make the little cat from simply patterned
fabric and tie a bow around its neck.

Row of
hearts
Make four
stuffed hearts.
Sew a loop at
the top of a
broad ribbon,
then sew the
hearts to the ribbon beneath it.

HANDY HINTS

This picture guide shows you all the useful craft and sewing skills that you need to make the projects in this book.

Drawing a circle

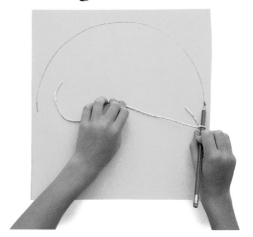

Tie a pencil to a piece of string. Hold the string where you want the center of the circle to be. Move the pencil around it, keeping the string taut.

Scoring a fold

1 To make a sharp fold in cardboard you must score the fold first. Hold a ruler along the fold and press the tip of your scissors along its edge.

2 Be careful not to cut right through the cardboard! Gently smooth the fold down flat along the scored line. The cardboard should fold over easily.

Drawing a square

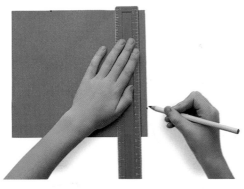

1 Starting from one corner of a piece of paper, measure along one edge and draw a dot. Then draw another dot the same distance along the other edge.

2 Imagine or draw a diagonal line between the two dots and fold the paper along it. Draw a dot at the corner of the folded paper, as shown.

3 Open the paper and join the center dot to the two dots at the edges of the paper. Cut along these two lines to make a perfect square.

Transferring a template

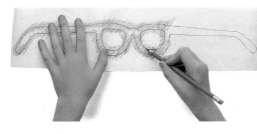

1 Trace the templates from the outlines on pages 62-63. Then, turn your tracing paper over and scribble over the back of it, as shown.

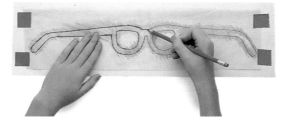

2 Turn the tracing paper back over and tape it onto some cardboard or thick paper, to hold it steady. Then carefully draw over your traced lines.

3 Remove the tracing paper. The scribbles will have transferred to the tracing to the paper below. Cut out the shape.

Using a sewing pattern

The templates for all the sewing projects are on pages 62-63. To make a pattern, trace the template you need onto a piece of tracing paper and cut it out. Then follow steps 1 and 2 to cut out the fabric pieces. When cutting out two pieces from a pattern, fold the fabric in half, right sides together, with the fabric design running straight up and down.

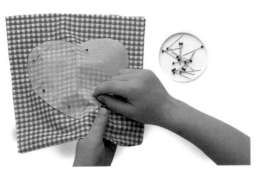 

1 Pin the pattern piece to the folded fabric, making sure that the pattern is lying straight along the fabric design, as shown.

2 Cut around the edge of the pattern piece. Turn the fabric as you cut, so that the scissors are always pointing away from you.

Trimming a seam

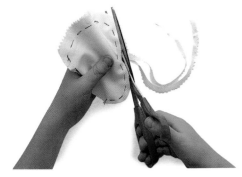

Trimming off the spare fabric around a seam makes the finished seam look neat. Cut halfway between the seam line and the edge, as shown.

Whipstitching a gap

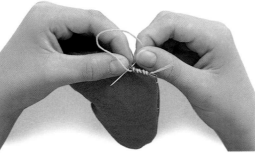 

1 Fold in the edges of the gap in the seam. Tie a knot in one end of the thread,★ then push the needle through both folded edges from back to front.

2 Take the needle around to the back again and repeat the stitch until the gap is closed.

Running stitch

Tie a knot in the end of the thread★ and push the needle through both pieces of fabric and back through to the front, as shown in step 1. Then pull the thread and the needle out through the fabric (step 2). Repeat steps 1 and 2 until you have finished the seam.

Backstitch

Tie a knot in the thread.★ Make the first stitch as for running stitch. Then put the needle through the hole at the end of the first stitch and up again a little way in front of the stitch you have just made, as shown in step 1. Repeat steps 1 and 2 until you have finished the seam.

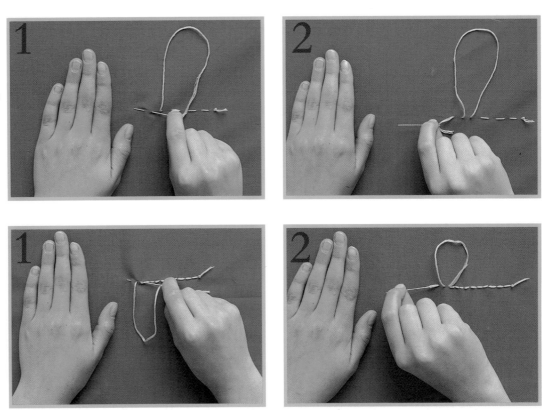

★For a strong seam, use a double thickness of ordinary sewing thread.

TEMPLATES

Here are the templates for the soft toys on pages 58-59, the disguises on pages 12-13, and the puppets on pages 44-45. You can find out how to make the templates and patterns on pages 60-61. Read the labels around the template you need before you start to make it.

Using a pattern

Using a pattern

Ask an adult to help you line up the top and bottom of each pattern with the grain of your fabric before pinning them both together.

Cutting line

Top

Cutting line

White rabbit's ears
Make a tracing paper pattern, as shown on page 61, then cut out two ears. Fold each ear in half along the dotted line and sew along the open sides, about $^{1}/_{2}$ in. (1 cm) in from the cut edge.

Fold line

Bottom

Top

Top

Cutting line

Fold line

Little cat
Make a tracing paper pattern, as shown on page 61. Fold a piece of fabric in half, right sides together, and pin the pattern to the fabric so that the dotted line lies along the fold. Cut the fabric out and then sew the open sides together, about $^{1}/_{2}$ in. (1 cm) in from the cut edge.

Bottom

Finger puppet template

Trace the pattern onto cardboard and cut it out, as shown
on page 60. Then look on page
44 for what to do next.

Cutting line

Cutting line

Dancing bear
or teddy

Make a tracing paper
pattern, as shown on
page 61. You will need
to cut out two pieces
of fabric for each bear.

Top

Bottom

Martha doll and white rabbit

Make a tracing paper pattern, as shown
on page 61. You will need to cut out two
pieces of fabric for each doll or rabbit.
Sew around the open sides, about $^1/_2$ in.
(1 cm) in from the cut edge.

Cutting line

Cutting line

Cutting line

Bottom

Eye patch

Trace the pattern onto
cardboard and cut it out,
as shown on page 60.
Then turn to page 12 to
find out what to do next.

Top

Soft heart

Make a tracing
paper pattern, as
shown on page
61. Cut out two
pieces of fabric
for each heart.

Cutting line

Glasses template

Make a template with wings for the
movie star shades or without the wings
for the disguise, as shown on page 60.

63

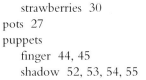

INDEX